Living the
Prophetic Life

J. Randolph Turpin, Jr.

Living the
Prophetic Life

J. Randolph Turpin, Jr.

DECLARATION PRESS

Living the Prophetic Life
Copyright © 2017 by J. Randolph Turpin, Jr.
All Rights Reserved

This material may not be reproduced in any form
without the expressed written permission of the author.

Scripture taken from the Holy Bible, New International Version®, NIV®. Copyright © 1973, 1978, 1984, 2011 by Biblica, Inc.™ Used by permission of Zondervan. All rights reserved worldwide. The "NIV" and "New International Version" are trademarks registered in the United States Patent and Trademark Office by Biblica, Inc.™

Scripture quotations taken from the New American Standard Bible® (NASB), Copyright © 1960, 1962, 1963, 1968, 1971, 1972, 1973, 1975, 1977, 1995 by The Lockman Foundation. Used by permission. www.Lockman.org.

Scripture taken from the Modern English Version®, MEV®. Copyright © 2014 by Military Bible Association. Used by permission. All rights reserved.

ISBN-10:0-9983102-1-2
ISBN-13:978-0-9983102-1-3

To my father,
Jim Turpin,
who taught me to listen.

Contents

Introduction		1
1	The Prophetic Anointing	7
2	Living Toward the Future	13
3	Living from Heaven	19
4	Living as an Agent of Change	25
5	Living by Revelation	33
6	Living from the Future	41
7	Living with Passion	47
8	Practices of the Prophetic Life	55
9	Challenges of the Prophetic Life	63
Conclusion		73
Reader's Reflections		75
Additional Resources		99

Introduction

Prophecy is powerful, but a prophetic life is more powerful. Imagine living a life that is fully oriented toward a hopeful future. Imagine approaching everything from heaven's point of view. Imagine being an agent of change sent by God to challenge the status quo. I am describing the prophetic life.

Much of what I do in this phase of my life is motivated by a passion to empower young adults to rise as a generation of revivalists. Most of my teaching pertains to Spirit-empowered ministry and the Spirit-empowered life. Many students at Valor Christian College in Columbus, Ohio have participated in my Essentials for Spirit-Empowered Ministry class where a great deal of this work takes place.

What God Is Doing

At a recent chapel service at the college, I presented three questions to the students, drawing their attention to what God had been doing among them. First, I asked, "How many of you this semester have received an authentic prophetic word from another student or from a professor that has changed your life?"

I was blessed to see the number of hands that went up. It has been very fulfilling to serve and lead in an environment where we as instructors have had the freedom to train students in the charismatic aspects of the Christian life. God is transforming and empowering their lives. They are learning how to follow the Spirit's leading in ministry, and they are experiencing an activation of their spiritual gifts.

In that chapel service, I also asked, "How many of you have been supernaturally healed through the ministry of your classmates this semester?"

Once again, a significant number of hands were raised. My mind went back to those moments over the preceding few weeks when I had been an eyewitness to a number of those healings. I am talking about instantaneous, verifiable miracles. In those instances, it was not my prayer or prophecy that released God's healing power. It was the ministry of these students!

Finally, I asked, "How many of you have experienced God performing these mighty works through *you* this semester?"

They raised their hands, confirming what I had seen with my own eyes. This testimony of Spirit-empowerment was overwhelming. In response to it all, we took a few moments to declare our praises to God, and we continue to give Him all of the glory.

It is my belief that this work taking place through our students at Valor Christian College is something that the Lord desires to activate through *all* believers. As I have said on many occasions, the supernatural is supposed to be normative for believers. For this reason, I have devoted my life to propagating the Spirit-empowered message. In this book, I especially want to motivate my readers to aspire to the *prophetic* aspects of the Spirit-empowered life.

Clarifying Our Terms

Before proceeding much further, I want to clarify what we mean by "prophecy" and "prophesy." For some, these terms immediately bring to mind end-time prophecies. Here we are not examining predictions leading to the return of Jesus or the end of the age. Rather, our study is related to the present-day function of the prophetic gifts as described in First Corinthians 12-14. Yet the reader should note that our greater concern is with *a way of life* associated with that gift-cluster. Better yet, it is a way of life accessible to *all* believers, whether they are greatly gifted prophetically or not.

What is the distinction between the words "prophecy" and "prophesy"? When these words are spoken, the difference between them is obvious. When read on the printed page, the distinction is sometimes missed. The word "prophecy" is a noun, and the word "prophesy" is a verb. Prophecy is the practice of prophesying.

There are three facets of meaning implied in the verb, "prophesy." First, to prophesy can mean to *forth-tell*—to speak forth the heart and mind of God. Second, to prophesy can mean to *fore-tell*—to speak of something before it happens. Third, to prophesy can mean to *speak for* another person—to speak as someone else's representative.

All three of these understandings are relevant to the Christian practice of prophesying. In short, prophecy is the vocal delivery of the heart and mind of the Father with a view toward a hopeful future.

In addition to the words "prophecy" and "prophesy," there is another term that you will encounter repeatedly; in fact, it is in the title of this book. What does the term, *"prophetic"* or *"the prophetic"* mean? Floyd McClung, former director of Youth With A Mission (YWAM), defines "the prophetic" as that *realm* where the natural interfaces with the supernatural.[1] It is God communicating with humans. Similarly, the adjective "prophetic" identifies *that which pertains to* the interface of the natural with the supernatural. It speaks of that which pertains to God

---

[1] Floyd McClung, "The Prophetic Journey," a prophetic ministry conference, 2005, Westmore Church of God, Cleveland, Tennessee.

communicating with mankind. Imagine the powerful implications of using that term as a descriptor of a quality of life—the prophetic life. We will unpack that thought later.

Our Approach

In the pages that follow, we will first consider a series of passages that deal with the prophetic anointing. I am going to make a particular emphasis based on those passages, but then I will shift the emphasis and apply it in a way that may seem a bit unusual to some. My initial focus will be on prophecy as defined above, but the emphasis will shift, taking the essence of the prophetic and applying it to the entirety of a person's life. The primary intent of this message is to promote *a way of life* that can be appropriately characterized as prophetic.

Reader's Reflections: Go to page 77 to note your initial reflections on this Introduction. What prayer or prophetic declaration would you like to make as you set forth to cultivate a prophetic life?

Living the Prophetic Life

Chapter One

The Prophetic Anointing

A study of the prophetic anointing could begin at a number of places in the Bible, but I have chosen to begin with one single verse in Numbers 11. Here in this section of Scripture, we join the Hebrews after their deliverance from Egypt. They are migrating to the Promised Land.

A Prophetic Leader

Up to this point, the people had become accustomed to the prophetic anointing resting upon one man—Moses. To a lesser degree, there were a few others (e.g., Aaron and Miriam) who had also functioned prophetically, but without a doubt, the focus was on Moses.

It is important to realize that there will always be a place for a strong prophetic leader in the midst of the church—a person upon whom the Spirit rests to lead prophetically and to empower God's people to function prophetically. Although this study is leading to a broader application of the prophetic, there is no intention here to detract from the essential role of a single prophetic leader. The inclusion of prophets in the Apostle Paul's list of five equipping gifts in Ephesians 4:11 highlights the importance of the prophet's function.

A Prophetic People

Although we are careful to affirm the unique role of the prophet, in Numbers 11 we see hints suggesting that the prophetic anointing would one day be released to *all* of God's people. In this narrative, the Lord took the same anointing that was on Moses and placed it on seventy elders. When that happened, some were concerned that individuals other than Moses were starting to prophesy, and they came to Moses complaining about it. It was then that Moses spoke these words: "Oh, that all the people of the Lord were prophets, and that the Lord would put His Spirit upon them!"[2]

Generations later, the prophet Joel foretold that this is precisely what would happen. The prophetic anointing was going to come on *all* the people of the Lord.[3]

In Acts 2, both Moses' desire and Joel's prophecy were fulfilled. On the Day of Pentecost, the Holy Spirit

---

[2] Numbers 11:29 (MEV).

[3] Joel 2:28-29.

was poured out upon the church, and the Apostle Peter quoted these words from the prophet Joel:

> "'In the last days it shall be,' says God,
> 'that I will pour out My Spirit on all flesh;
> your sons and your daughters shall prophesy,
> your young men shall see visions,
> and your old men shall dream dreams.
> Even on My menservants and maidservants
> I will pour out My Spirit in those days;
> and they shall prophesy.'"[4]

Prophecy became an emphasis in the Early Church. We see that emphasis in the Apostle Paul's correspondence with the church in Corinth. In First Corinthians 14:1, he said, "Follow after love and desire spiritual gifts, but especially that you may prophesy."

Much of First Corinthians 14 continues with the emphasis on Spirit-empowered prophecy. Verse 26 indicates that prophecy contributes to the edification of people. Verse 31 suggests that *all* can potentially prophesy. Throughout the chapter, Paul gives a great deal of instruction to ensure that the prophetic would function properly in the church.

The Quality of the Prophetic Anointing

God is essentially and entirely good, and all that He speaks is good. When He anoints a prophetic person to speak on His behalf, that person is

---

[4] Acts 2:17-18 (MEV).

authorized and empowered to represent Him. Both the content of the message and the manner of delivery are to mirror His heart. Authentic prophecy releases the goodness of God.

Scripture defines the needed qualities for stewarding the prophetic anointing. Everything prophetic should be handled and delivered with love. To the Corinthians, Paul said, "If I have the gift of prophecy, and understand all mysteries and all knowledge,... and have not love, I am nothing."[5]

Love compels prophetic people to act and speak in a way that releases God's goodness into situations where the revelation of His heart is needed. Paul makes this emphasis in First Corinthians 14:3, saying, "But he who prophesies speaks to men for their edification and exhortation and comfort."[6] In some versions of this passage, the word "edification" is translated "strengthening," and the word "exhortation" is translated "encouragement."

Think of the potential impact. When the prophetic anointing is stewarded in love and in recognition of God's goodness, the result will be this effect: somebody is going to be built up. The weak will be made strong. Those who are in sorrow will be comforted. The discouraged will suddenly find that courage has been imparted to them. They will be

---

[5] 1 Corinthians 13:2 (MEV).

[6] 1 Corinthians 14:3 (MEV).

supernaturally encouraged by what they hear, and they will be less likely to fall into sin, because Hebrews 3:13 implies that encouraged people are less likely to be hardened by sin's deceitfulness. Can you see why people operating under an authentic prophetic anointing tend to be healthier and stronger?

I cannot help but get excited about the possibilities for transformation that accompany a people living under the prophetic anointing. In the power of the Spirit, you are authorized and empowered to speak words that deliver the heart of the Father into the lives of others—words that build up, comfort, instill courage and strengthen. When you prophesy, the very words that you speak represent the sound and life of heaven.

A Shift in Focus

Now I want to shift the focus a bit. There is one aspect of our life in the Spirit that is far more important than prophesying. It includes prophesying, but it is something more. We have talked about our words delivering the heart and mind of the Father with a view toward a hopeful future. Such is the essence of prophecy. Prophetic utterances are powerful, but let us take this further.

If *our words* can deliver the Father's heart and mind, what would it look like if *our lives*—everything about our lives—delivered the heart and mind of the Father with a view toward a hopeful future? Ponder this thought. Aspire to live this kind of life. I want to stir you up to live the prophetic life.

Reader's Reflections: Go to page 79 to note your reflections on the Prophetic Anointing. What prayer do you want to pray? What prophetic declaration do you want to make?

Chapter Two

Living Toward the Future

All that natural man[7] can comprehend are memories of the *past* and perceptions of the *present*. Comprehension of *future* realities requires revelation. The good news is that we who are indwelt by the Holy Spirit are not limited to that which is natural. As sons and daughters of God, we are a people made for future realities.

Our Father delights in giving us glimpses of futuristic things. In Scripture we have His revelation of our ultimate glorification. We are also told in the written word of things that are yet to come upon the earth. In addition to the objective, biblical documentation of revelations that were given long ago, we also have ongoing subjective means for viewing the unseen future through dreams, visions and the

---

[7] References to "natural man" and "spiritual man" are made in the gender-neutral sense.

charismatic, revelatory gifts.[8] By His grace, God has given us the ability to orient our lives toward the future and to pursue that future with great confidence and faith.

Do Not Look Back

The prophetic life is future-oriented. Do not look back! Your life is not to be governed by the past or even by the present. We have been blessed with a life governed and influenced by the future, and that future is glorious. The Apostle Paul made this emphasis when he wrote to the Philippians, saying,

> Brothers, I do not count myself to have attained, but this one thing I do, forgetting those things which are behind and reaching forward to those things which are ahead, I press toward the goal to the prize of the high calling of God in Christ Jesus.[9]

Review the passage once again, and take note of the "one thing" Paul said that he does. What is that "one thing"?

What we see in the Philippians 3 passage is one simple instruction that will bring us nearer to the fulfillment of what Paul regarded as life's highest

---

[8] The charismatic, revelatory gifts presented in First Corinthians 12-14 are the word of knowledge, the word of wisdom and the discerning of spirits.

[9] Philippians 3:13-14 (MEV).

ambition. That ambition is depicted a few verses earlier when he said,

> I consider everything a loss because of the surpassing worth of knowing Christ Jesus my Lord,.... I want to know Christ—yes, to know the power of his resurrection and participation in his sufferings, becoming like him in his death, and so, somehow, attaining to the resurrection from the dead.[10]

For Paul, life's highest ambition was "to know Christ," and his "one thing" was to "press toward" the fulfillment of that one ambition.

Take yet another look at the Philippians 3 passage. Note that the "one thing" actually involves two actions taken together: *forgetting* the past and *reaching forward* to the future. Living toward the future requires *forgetting* some things that are in the past. The context suggests here that forgetting the past means to no longer be influenced or controlled by the past.

There are a number of things that believers should refuse to allow their minds to dwell upon. Refuse to look back at sins that your Father has already forgiven. Refuse to look back at past defeats. Refuse to look back at conflicts that stir up negative feelings toward others. Refuse to look back at decisions that cannot be changed. Refuse to look back thinking that the past was better than it really was. Refuse to look back at

---

[10] Philippians 3:8-11 (NIV).

past victories and successes, thinking that your best days are behind you.[11]

As appropriate as these refusals are, Paul had yet another thing in mind when he spoke of "forgetting those things which are behind." In the context of Philippians 3:4-6, it is clear that Paul wanted to forget all of his previous religious accomplishments—all of the works that he erroneously had thought were placing him in good standing before God. It was all worthless compared to Christ. He was more than ready to leave it all behind for the sake of pressing "toward the goal to the prize of the high calling of God in Christ Jesus."[12]

Forget, and let go of all of these hindrances. Do not look back. None of it is worth another moment's consideration. God's will and reward are in front of you, not behind you.

Move Forward with Hope

A prophetic life moves forward with *hope*. Before Christianity's influence on the word, "hope" simply meant "expectation." In some instances, it meant an expectation for something good, but at other times it

---

[11] This list of refusals is based in part on a list used by numerous preachers and writers, including Kieran Beville, Joseph Hovsepian, C. J. Jackson and Terrell D. Davis. The original author of the list may have been Roger Campbell.

[12] Philippians 3:14 (MEV).

could even mean an expectation for something unfavorable. The context determined its meaning. After Christianity's influence, "hope" came to mean "expectation of good" or "expectation of a favorable outcome." Prophetic living is oriented toward a hopeful future where the goodness of God is anticipated.

The prophetic life is lived with the expectation that things promised will come to pass. I am talking about things promised in Scripture and things promised through prophetic revelation. Prophetic living holds to that which is not yet as though it were already so. Such a life is in perfect alignment with God's kingdom, for the peculiar nature of the kingdom is that it is "already, but not yet."

A prophetic life does not accept hardship, limitation or apparent impossibility as the final word. When everyone else is giving up, the person living prophetically cannot imagine quitting. Prophetic people see situations in terms of what *can* be and what *will* be. They see people in the same light. When we function out of a prophetic mindset, we esteem people for what they are becoming, not just for what they are.

Move forward with hope. Remember all that God has promised you. Step through the barriers of apparent impossibility. Live toward your destiny. Never shrink back. Resist the lies, and embrace the fullness of the truth contained in these words: "He

Living the Prophetic Life

who began a good work in you will carry it on to completion until the day of Christ Jesus."[13]

Reader's Reflections: Go to page 81 to note your reflections concerning Living Toward the Future. What future-oriented prayer do you want to pray? What prophetic declaration do you want to make?

---

[13] Philippians 1:6 (NIV).

Chapter Three

Living from Heaven

The prophetic life is a kind of life that brings into this world a constant manifestation of heaven. Such is the way that Jesus lived when He walked this planet, and since He is our model for everything, we are to live the same way. Our union with Him makes living from heaven possible.

My use of this expression, "living from heaven," may not initially make sense to you. Obviously, we are still on earth, so how can we possibly live from heaven? The possibility of a life lived from heaven begins to unfold when we review how Jesus taught His disciples to pray. Follow my line of reasoning, and you will soon see the beauty of this truth.

One day Jesus' disciples observed the way that their Master prayed. When He finished praying, they made this request: "Lord, teach us to pray."[14]

---

[14] Luke 11:1 (MEV).

In response, Jesus said,

"When you pray, say:
Our Father, who is in heaven,
hallowed be Your name.
Your kingdom come;
Your will be done on earth, as it is in heaven."[15]

The prayer has several more lines, but we will stop here to draw out a portion of the truth supporting the idea of a "from heaven" kind of life.

First, note that heaven is mentioned twice in this verse. The Father is identified as being *in heaven*, and the prayer implies that the will of God needed on earth is already established *in heaven*. Consider what heaven is. It is a place of perfection. There is no sin or affliction in heaven. There is no death, sorrow or pain in heaven. The holy presence of God is fully manifested in heaven. Even though I have never seen heaven with my physical eyes, I could write many more pages describing the celestial realm based on what the Bible tells us about it.

Second, let us consider the Greek word order in the final line of verse two. Word order is important in Greek, for the order of words often indicates the intended emphasis. In our English translations, the line reads, "Your will be done on earth, as it is in heaven." In the Greek text it reads, "Your will be done, as in heaven, even so on earth."

---

[15] Luke 11:2 (MEV).

What difference does this word order make? As suggested above, there is a difference in emphasis. If I am praying for God's will to be done on earth, as it is in heaven, I am beginning my prayer from the vantage point of earth. I am beginning with the troubles of earth, and with my prayer I am trying to lift my troubles to heaven to get heaven's answer to my petition. In a sense, my experience on earth is setting the agenda for my prayer and for how I am conducting myself as I approach heaven's throne.

With the word order found in the original language, my prayer does *not* begin from the vantage point of earth. It begins from the vantage point of heaven. The prayer is, "As in heaven, even so on earth." When I pray in this manner, the troubles of earth do not set the agenda for my prayer or for how I approach the throne. The bliss of heaven sets the agenda! I begin at the throne! In fact, I am already seated at the throne!

Remember, the Bible says that God has "raised us up and seated us together in heavenly places in Christ Jesus."[16] Where is Jesus seated? He is seated at the Father's right hand,[17] and we are right there with Him. Just as sure as I am physically seated in Columbus, Ohio typing these words, I am also spiritually seated in heavenly places in Christ Jesus. That seat is the place

---

[16] Ephesians 2:6 (MEV).

[17] Ephesians 1:20.

from which I pray, it is the position from which I prophesy, and it is the seat from which I live my life.

This change of perspective has powerful implications. When I was praying from earth to heaven, I was praying *for* my breakthrough. Now that I am praying from heaven to earth, I am praying *from* my breakthrough. The same applies to the way that I conduct myself in all other aspects of my life. Prophetic living is lived from heaven to earth.

Pastor Rod Parsley of World Harvest Church in Columbus, Ohio presents a similar truth when he speaks of praying and living from a place of God's presence. At times people fall short of experiencing the breakthrough they need because they do not begin their praying by first making themselves aware of God's presence. When we live and pray from the presence of God, we live and pray from a place of an authority that has already been established and a victory that has already been won.

Bill Johnson of Bethel Church in Redding, California has greatly influenced my thinking on this subject. His book entitled *When Heaven Invades Earth*,[18] is a "must read" item for any person wanting to live the kind of life I am describing. The words that follow are my paraphrase of what Bill Johnson teaches

---

[18] Bill Johnson, *When Heaven Invades Earth: A Practical Guide to a Life of Miracles* (Shippensburg, Pennsylvania: Destiny Image Publishers, 2005).

repeatedly. If there is no sin, no affliction, no oppression and no poverty in heaven, then those things should not be on earth either.

As a person devoted to living a prophetic life, I am fully authorized and empowered to discern the will of God as established in heaven and pray it into the earth. Likewise, I am authorized and empowered to *live* the life of heaven as I fulfill my days on earth.

May we become increasingly aware of the heavenly realm. I even dare to pray to become *more* aware of the heavenly than I am aware of the earthly. Such a desire is in keeping with what Paul meant when he said, "Set your minds on things above, not on earthly things."[19]

Reader's Reflections: Go to page 83 to note your reflections concerning Living from Heaven. Knowing that you are living from your breakthrough rather than for your breakthrough, what prayer do you want to pray? What prophetic declaration do you want to make?

---

[19] Colossians 3:2 (NIV).

Living the Prophetic Life

Chapter Four

Living as an Agent of Change

When people, systems, cultures and situations need transformation, the desired change is unlikely to take place through external force and manipulation. There is a place for external legislation and regulation, but the changes that God wants to see require something more—even something better. The solution is the prophetic infusion of the kingdom of heaven.

People who live prophetically are agents of change. They represent the kingdom of heaven, and the introduction of that kingdom disturbs things that are not compatible with it. The prophetic disrupts the status quo and calls for alignment with heaven's order.

As a prophetic person, *you* represent that kingdom. *You* have been authorized to introduce the ways of heaven into the earth. Consequently, your presence in any environment constitutes a call to heaven's purposes. Through you God will release His love, peace and presence. With that release, He may also manifest prophetic words and actions to activate change. All of this activity will result in God's goodness being revealed in the places where He sends you.

Prophetic Tension

While living a prophetic life, your presence may cause some to feel uncomfortable. You are likely to be perceived as an anomaly—something other than what is expected. At times you may feel that you do not belong in this world, and others may feel that way about you too.

No one should regard this awkward dynamic as a license or excuse for being weird. We need to responsibly manage ourselves in our social interactions so that we do not unnecessarily shut down opportunities to be a godly influence in society. Neither should this awkwardness be despised. It is one of the evidences that people and systems around us are being summoned to heaven's order.

Part of this awkward feeling is due to the fact that the prophetic life is future-oriented. As a prophetic person, you are living a life that is somewhat ahead of its time. For this reason, often you will be misunderstood. What is obvious to you will not be obvious to others, because your gaze is fixed on what *can* be and *will* be. You are holding on to things that cannot be seen and things that are not yet. You are living life with a willingness to be a sign of God's intentions in the earth.

As a prophetic person, God will place you in the middle of situations for the purpose of creating a tension. It is a healthy and needed tension. Without that tension, there would be little hope for change. It is a tension between what *is* and what *ought* to be. It is a tension between the *present situation* and the *preferred future*. It might also be a tension between *injustice* and *justice*, between *evil* and *good*, or between the *unholy* and the *holy*.

Although this tension can lead to negative reactions, it often results in positive emotional responses from the people affected. For instance, you may find yourself in the midst of complacent people, and initially you will cause them to feel uncomfortable, because the Spirit that you carry is not complacent. By simply walking into the room, you will spur them on to greatness. You may show up in the midst of hatred, and with a single word or action, anger will lose its power, for the Spirit that you carry is the personification of love. You may find yourself in a context of strife and hostility, and through you, God will frustrate the spirits inciting turmoil. Peace will come in its place. You may step into a gathering of people full of doubt, fear and confusion, and through you the very presence of Jesus will come to contradict those negative emotions.

Prophetic Influence

In this study, we have already reviewed First Corinthians 14:3 as a description of the positive effect

Living the Prophetic Life

of a spoken prophetic word. When we *speak* prophetically from the heart of the Father, people are built up, strengthened, encouraged and comforted. The same thing can happen when we *live* prophetically. When the prophetic is understood to be more than the act of prophesying and is applied to the way that we live our lives, we move into what I will here call "prophetic influence."

When we carry the qualities that manifest edification, strengthening, encouragement and comfort,[20] we become agents of prophetic influence. Change occurs. People who have been torn down are built back up. The weak are made strong. Those who are discouraged find that their courage has been revived. The lonely and the sorrowful are comforted.

In light of First Corinthians 14:3, the key elements of prophetic influence are edification (i.e., strengthening), encouragement and comfort. There is much more implied in these elements than meets the eye. For instance, think about what it means to edify or

---

[20] Up to this point, I have been speaking of *four functions* of *prophetic utterance,* and here in our discussion on prophetic living, I have been presenting them as *four elements* of *prophetic influence.* In First Corinthians 14:3, there are actually only three elements listed: edification, encouragement and comfort. Because the Greek word translated "edification" has also been rendered as "strengthening" by some, I have been speaking of it as "edification and strengthening."

build up a person. How does edification happen? What does it look like? Time and space does not permit us to do so, but here is where I would love to interject an in-depth study of the numerous "one another" teachings of the Bible, to see how powerfully we as Christians can build others up through the way that we interact with them.

To note a few of the "one another" exhortations, consider what happens when we "honor one another"[21]—acknowledge the value of others. Consider what happens when we "pray for one another."[22] Consider what happens when we "spur one another on toward love and good deeds."[23]

Furthermore, consider what happens when we do all of this with an awareness that we bring the presence of God and joy into the situation. In His presence there is fullness of joy,[24] and the joy of the Lord is our strength.[25] It is in such presence-centered, joyful encounters with people and situations that the strengthening aspect of edification is realized.

---

[21] Romans 12:10 (NIV).

[22] James 5:16 (MEV).

[23] Hebrews 10:24 (NIV).

[24] Psalm 16:11 (KJV).

[25] Nehemiah 8:10 (KJV).

Most of us think of our role as change agents in terms of how our lives might positively influence individuals or groups of people. Yes, directly touching the lives of *people* must remain our priority, but I also want to encourage you to get a bigger vision of the power of your life. Think in terms of the spheres of influence in society and culture.

What impact might a prophetic life have in the realm of the arts and entertainment? What difference might a prophetic life make in the world of business, science and technology? How about the field of education? What about family services? Have you considered politics and government? How about media and communications? Last but not least, do you think that a prophetic influence might make a difference in the realm of religion?

Some might say, "Oh, but it is too dark in those places!" Really? Do you really think that the darkness is more powerful than the light? Does darkness stand a chance against light? I have never had to push darkness out of a room before flipping a light switch. The light comes on, and the darkness is gone. Some of you have been resisting your calling into those darkened places. Realize who and whose you are. You are a son or daughter of the Light. Think about it, and remember that you are an agent of change.

Reader's Reflections: Go to page 85 to note your reflections concerning Living as an Agent of Change. In what ways can you relate to the concepts of prophetic tension and prophetic influence mentioned in this chapter? In light of these realities, what prayer do you want to pray? What prophetic declaration do you want to make?

Living the Prophetic Life

Chapter Five

Living by Revelation

Life can be lived by reason or by revelation. Both are needed in a Christian's life, but which of the two will we allow to lead the way? By reason, we can assess a situation and make a judgment call based on that assessment. However, while the engaging of reason is a vital aspect of a Christian's thinking, it does have limitations:

1. Reason cannot access knowledge of the future.
2. Reason cannot access knowledge of the spiritual forces and realities at work.
3. Reason alone cannot always rightly discern the will of God.
4. Reason alone does not engage God relationally as decisions are being made.

Western Christianity seems to have little difficulty in embracing reason as a way of knowing, but the possibility of contemporary revelation is often met with suspicion. The conveyance of knowledge through preaching or teaching is readily welcomed, but the prophetic is often categorically held at a distance.

There is a great need in the church for people who will live and lead by revelation. Revelation is needed because the agenda for heaven's purposes should not be set by natural factors. Only God determines that agenda. The ongoing and ultimate question for the Christian is this: "What is the will of God?"

Although spiritual realities need to be engaged intellectually, they can only be comprehended spiritually. Paul made this emphasis when he wrote to the Corinthians, saying,

> The man without the Spirit does not accept the things that come from the Spirit of God, for they are foolishness to him, and he cannot understand them, because they are spiritually discerned. The spiritual man makes judgments about all things, but he himself is not subject to any man's judgment: "For who has known the mind of the Lord that he may instruct him?" But we have the mind of Christ.[26]

How does spiritual understanding come to us? A few verses earlier, Paul says,

> However, as it is written: "No eye has seen, no ear has heard, no mind has conceived what God has prepared for those who love him"—but God has

---

[26] 1 Corinthians 2:14-16 (NIV).

revealed it to us by his Spirit. The Spirit searches all things, even the deep things of God.[27]

The understanding that we need comes supernaturally. It comes by revelation through the Holy Spirit. Back up a little further in chapter two, and Paul tells us why God has chosen to manifest such understanding solely through the Spirit:

> When I came to you, brothers, I did not come with eloquence or superior wisdom as I proclaimed to you the testimony about God. For I resolved to know nothing while I was with you except Jesus Christ and him crucified. I came to you in weakness and fear, and with much trembling. My message and my preaching were not with wise and persuasive words, but with a demonstration of the Spirit's power, so that your faith might not rest on men's wisdom, but on God's power.[28]

Here it is clearly stated. God does not want our faith to be based in human reason. Our faith is to rest on God's power.

Reliance on Divine Guidance

The prophetic life is intentionally dependent on divine guidance. Those who live this kind of life want to feel what God is feeling, think what God is thinking, go where God is going, do what God is doing and say what God is saying. Such a life is made possible by the

---

[27] 1 Corinthians 2:9-10 (NIV).

[28] 1 Corinthians 2:1-5 (NIV).

Holy Spirit who indwells us. Sensitivity to the leading of the Spirit is a core value for the person desiring to live the prophetic life.

The prophetic life is guided supernaturally. As we conduct ourselves in the affairs of life and ministry, we are not just responding to what everybody around us wants. We are not reacting to popular opinion. We are not even allowing apparent needs to determine what we do, though responding to needs is important. As prophetic people, we rely upon divine guidance.

Jesus set the example for us in this area. In John 5:19, Jesus said, "I tell you the truth, the Son can do nothing by himself; he can do only what he sees his Father doing, because whatever the Father does the Son also does."[29]

Jesus was and is God in the flesh, yet He said that He could do nothing by himself. Even Jesus relied upon divine guidance. If Jesus, the Son of God, needed revelatory direction, how much more so do we need it.

When Jesus showed up on the scene, He did not just walk around and start randomly working miracles. First, He made himself aware of what the Father was doing and what the Father was saying. Once He discerned the will of His Father, then He aligned His actions and words accordingly. We are to do the same.

---

[29] John 5:19 (NIV).

Often when I walk into a room, I ask Holy Spirit, "What is the Father doing right now?" Sometimes I hear nothing in response, but often He will highlight someone to me or whisper a word of prophetic guidance. At times the answer comes as a *feeling*—a sense of what is going on in the spiritual atmosphere. On some occasions, the Spirit's response comes in the form of a divine appointment: He sets me up for a conversation or for some deed of kindness. If you are not already doing so, I would encourage you to start asking for revelation of what the Father is prepared to do in the settings where you find yourself.

An Appetite for God's Word

A prophetic life is lived on the basis of every word that comes from the mouth of God. When Jesus was tempted by Satan toward the end of a forty-day fast, he responded to the tempter with three "it is written" statements.[30] In other words, Jesus wielded the sword of the Spirit—the word of God.[31] It is the first of those three statements that I want to ponder.

Consider the situation. Jesus was hungry because He had not eaten in over a month, so Satan tried to convince Him to turn stones into bread. It was then that Jesus quoted from the book of Deuteronomy, saying, "It is written, 'Man shall not live by bread

---

[30] Matthew 4:1-11.

[31] Ephesians 6:17.

alone, but by every word that proceeds out of the mouth of God.'"[32]

What are we to learn from these words? If we are relying on natural means alone (i.e., bread) to sustain our lives, we will not survive. Our life depends on "every word that proceeds out of the mouth of God."

In one sense, Jesus is talking about the already-written word of God as recorded in the Bible. In another sense, He is talking about *any* word that God speaks, whether it be through Scripture or through prophetic revelation. Whichever way it comes to us, our lives are to be lived on the basis of hearing from God and acting on what is heard.

As a prophetic people, we live by the sound of God's voice—what He says and what He reveals. I am talking about a life that is lived on the basis of every word that comes out of God's mouth.

I want to stir you up with this point. Just as you would have an appetite for physical bread, live your life with an appetite for every word that comes from the mouth of God. Live your life with a hunger for anything and everything that He speaks. Then every time He speaks to you, devour those words like you would devour your favorite meal, and keep yourself in a place of hunger for more. Our attitude should be one

---

[32] Matthew 4:4 (MEV), quoting Deuteronomy 8:3.

that says, "I can't wait for the next thing He has to say to me! I live to hear the sound of His voice!"

When you have an appetite for what God has to say, it brings life to you. It always brings life. When you eat bread, it is life-giving to the body. When you devour the word of God, it is life-giving to the spirit, soul *and* body. There is nothing else that can satisfy like the sound of His voice.

There have been many times in my life when I have said to my wife, "All we need right now is one word. All we need to settle this situation is one word from God." We would go into prayer, and we would wait before the Lord. Then the prophetic word would come, awakening us to the possibilities of what God would be pleased to do in the situation. With just one word, the matter would be settled.

A good way to cultivate an appetite for the sound of God's voice is to daily become immersed in the reading of the Bible. As you read, you will occasionally come upon moments when it seems that the words are jumping off of the page and into your heart. Mark what that feels like. In such moments, you are hearing the voice of God. Over time, you will start noticing that you are hearing that same voice even when you are not reading your Bible. When people become aware that they are hearing the sound of God's voice, it is then that they get an appetite for more.

Living the Prophetic Life

Reader's Reflections: Go to page 87 to note your reflections concerning Living by Revelation. How can you cultivate a greater sensitivity to God's voice? With this emphasis in mind, what prayer do you want to pray? What prophetic declaration do you want to make?

Chapter Six

Living from the Future

The title of this chapter may seem as strange to you as the chapter entitled, "Living from Heaven," presented earlier. The title may also seem to contradict the chapter entitled, "Living Toward the Future," presented earlier. Actually, the prophetic life is lived both toward and from the future, but the "from the future" aspect obviously requires explanation.

An Unlimited God

To arrive at an understanding of this idea of living from the future, let us begin with this truth: God is unlimited. He is not limited by anything in His universe; He created all of it, and He is sovereign. He is not limited by space, and He is not limited by time.

There are a number of references in the Bible that back up my claim that God is not limited by time. In the days of Joshua, when God gave the Amorites over to Israel, He caused the sun and moon to "stand still," allowing more time for Israel's enemies to be defeated.[33] In the days of King Hezekiah, God set time back ten degrees on the sundial as a sign that He was going to heal the king.[34] He is the Lord over time.

God exists both inside of time and outside of time. He is eternal. He is still in your *past*; He is most certainly in your *present*; and He is already in your *future*. He can be present at all points in time simultaneously. In contrast, Satan is *not* omnipresent. He is *not* already in your future. He does *not* have the same view of your life that God has. These truths have powerful ramifications for the prophetic life.

Thinking and Praying Outside of Time

People living a prophetic life think differently, speak differently and pray differently. Praying to a God who exists outside of time can have some astounding results. A number of years ago I served as the administrator of a small Christian school in Maine. The founders were committed to running the school by faith. When families could not afford the tuition, we would often allow students to enroll for whatever lesser amount parents were able to pay.

One week I realized that we did not have enough money in the school's account to pay what we owed our vendors. On the day that one of the bills was due, I

---

[33] Joshua 10:12-14.

[34] 2 Kings 20:8-11 and Isaiah 38:7-8.

Living from the Future

drove to the post office to check the mail. When I stepped out of my car and started walking toward the post office door, I prayed, "Father, this bill is due today. We do not have the money to pay it. I know that you are unlimited by time, so, I am asking you to *reach back three days ago* and place it on somebody's heart to send us a check for this amount of money."

I walked into the post office, opened the school's post office box, and there it was! It was a letter from someone with whom we seldom had contact, and they had enclosed a check for the precise amount to pay the bill that was due that day!

The story I have just shared is an example of not allowing even time to be a limitation. It is what I call "praying outside of time." Yet a greater example is found in the ministry of Jesus. Follow me as I walk through part of the narrative of John 16 and 17.

In John 16 we meet up with Jesus and His disciples prior to Him praying the great prayer of John 17. Note that Jesus had not yet died on the cross. He had not yet been raised from the dead. He had not yet been glorified. He had not yet defeated death, hell and the grave. Yet He spoke these words:

> "These things I have spoken to you, so that in Me you may have peace. In the world you have tribulation, but take courage; I have overcome the world."[35]

---

[35] John 16:33 (NASB).

Do you see what is happening here? Jesus said, "I *have* overcome the world," *before* His cross-death, resurrection and glorification! He said, "I *have* overcome the world," *before* He had overcome it! Jesus was thinking and speaking outside of time!

Now, move down the page a little further and into the prayer that Jesus prayed in John 17. Look at verse 11. In the middle of His prayer, Jesus says to His Father,

> "I am no longer in the world; and yet they themselves are in the world, and I come to You."[36]

Does anything appear strange to you about this passage? A number of versions mistranslate what Jesus says here, rendering the words as "I am to be no longer in the world,"[37] or "I will remain in the world no longer."[38] The original language really does say, "I *am* no longer in the world," even though *He was still in the world*. Jesus' feet were still on planet earth. He was still standing among His disciples, yet He said, "I am no longer in the world." I think that some translators looked at the Greek text and said, "This makes no sense. This can't mean what it looks like it means." So, they modified it a bit to make the words fit within our normal way of thinking.

---

[36] John 17:11 (NASB).

[37] John 17:11 (MEV).

[38] John 17:11 (NIV).

What is the point? Jesus was praying outside of time! Yes, *in His body*, Jesus was still in this world. His feet were still on the earth, and He was still standing among His disciples. Yet *in spirit*, in this time of prayer, He was no longer in this world! He had already arrived in heaven! He was standing in the presence of His Father! His victory had already been accomplished! What was Jesus doing? In spirit, He had placed himself at the vantage point of the future and was looking back on the present situation. From that point of view, Jesus spoke of those things that were not yet manifested as though they were.[39]

Jesus thought, prophesied and prayed outside of time. If He is our model for everything, then we are given an implied permission to do the same. Prophetic thinking and praying is about placing yourself in the vantage point of your future and looking back on your situation.

What is the pressing need that you are currently bringing to the Father in prayer? Ask Holy Spirit to give you a vision or picture of that situation totally resolved. Once you receive that image, in spirit, place yourself in the middle of that answered prayer, and look back on the present. Then from the vantage point of the future, start making prophetic declarations over your present. Bring your petition to the Father, believe that you *have* received it, and, as Jesus promised, it will

---

[39] Romans 4:17.

be yours.[40] Even now, start offering expressions of thanksgiving to God for what He *has* done even *before* He has done it!

I really believe that when we get in the spirit, we are connected with an eternal realm that is not limited by time and space. In those moments, we are connected with eternity, and we have the opportunity to experience God's perspective on every situation. Such is the way that prophetic people live from their future.

Reader's Reflections: Go to page 89 to note your reflections concerning Living from the Future. Ask Holy Spirit to allow you to look back on your present situation from a future vantage point—from a future point in time where your breakthrough will already be accomplished. From that future point of view, what prayer do you want to pray into your present situation? What prophetic declaration do you want to make?

---

[40] Mark 11:24.

Chapter Seven

Living with Passion

People living the prophetic life typically are not individuals who began this journey by setting their aim toward the prophetic. From the start, the centering of their heart was upon Jesus. Their great desire was to know Him deeply. Nothing else would satisfy.

The prophetic life is more concerned about *intimacy* with God than *power* with Him. Power with God is vital to our mission; and power with God will come; but it will flow out of a passionate heart-to-heart relationship. Power is found in knowing Him.

There are numerous facets to this divine-human connection. In some contexts, it is a relationship between a benevolent Master and a servant. We could speak of this bond as a friendship; we could speak of it in terms of the love between a Father and His child; but there is no metaphor more powerful than the imagery of the divine romance—the love between the heavenly Bridegroom and His bride.

Jesus and His Bride

In 1995, our congregation in the Portland, Maine area partnered with the local Vineyard Christian Fellowship and invited Mike Bickle, founder of Kansas City's International House of Prayer, to come for an entire week to teach from Solomon's Song of Songs.[41] I had read through and studied this Song many times, but that week it affected me like never before. A year earlier I had been overtaken by a new-found intimacy with Jesus, but Bickle's "Passion for Jesus" message drew me even deeper into it.

The Song of Songs is a celebration of married love, but it is also much more. Once we get past the literal content of the text and tap into its symbolism, we discover an awe-inspiring revelation of the relationship between Jesus and His bride—the relationship between Jesus and all who are devoted to Him.[42] Through the imagery of this marvelous Song, we see the heavenly Bridegroom pursuing us, and then we see our pursuit of Him. As we follow the story, we get caught up in the all-consuming nature of this romance. If you are after God's heart, one of the best things you can do to become more passionate and

---

[41] In some versions of the Bible, the Song of Songs is called the Song of Solomon.

[42] Even pre-Christian Jews understood the Song of Songs to be a song about the relationship between God and His people, Israel.

intimate in your relationship with Christ is to immerse yourself in a reflective study of this Song.

While keeping the bridal paradigm in mind, let us also consider for a few moments another aspect of this heart-to-heart connection. Several descriptors could be helpful for comprehending the passion of this relationship, but here we will mention only one more. We are to live as *friends* of God.

Friends of God

One of the names for the Son of God is the name "Emmanuel"—meaning, "God is with us." Ever since the expulsion of Adam and Eve from the Garden of Eden, the Lord has greatly desired to once again dwell with man. He longs for friendship with us. It boggles the mind when one realizes that this great God actually *wants* to be close to us.

Like Abraham, the desire of many believers is to be called the "friend of God." The desire is reciprocal: God also wants to be friends with us. Yes, He wants our obedience too, but He so greatly longs for obedience rising out of a passion for Him and His Son.

While many desire to be busy about our Master's business, let us not forget the lesson portrayed by the story of Mary and Martha in Luke 10:38-42 where Mary sat at the feet of Jesus clinging to His every word while Martha was busy about her work. Yes, there is work to be done, but what the Savior desires from us more than anything else is the kind of passion that

Mary had for His presence.[43] It is out of our intimacy with the Lord that the prophetic life will flow.[44]

Pursue intimacy with Christ. The prophetic life is more about a deeper relational intimacy with God than it is about receiving specific revelatory details and knowledge. Jack Deere, the author of *Surprised by the Voice of God*, states, "Friendship is the key to recognizing God's voice."[45]

Jesus called His disciples into an intimate friendship with himself. In His earliest days with these young followers, He summoned them to be *with* Him before He ever released them to minister in authority and power.[46] Intimate communion with Jesus is a prerequisite to effectiveness and integrity in Spirit-empowered ministry. Jesus would eventually commission these disciples to proclaim the Gospel and demonstrate its power, but first, they needed an extended season of living every moment in His

---

[43] Luke 10:38-42.

[44] To accentuate the emphasis already made in the main body of this text, those who want to explore the subject of intimacy with God and passion for Jesus further should study Solomon's Song of Songs from the allegorical perspective.

[45] Jack Deere, *Surprised by the Voice of God: How God Speaks Today through Prophecies, Dreams, and Visions* (Grand Rapids, Michigan: Zondervan Publishing House, 1996), 331.

[46] Mark 3:13-15.

company, absorbing His words and coming to know His heart. There was a mystical dimension to this relationship; although Jesus and His disciples would one day be physically separated from one another, in reality, He would never leave them.

Jesus wants more from us than mere work or service. He truly wants *friendship* with us. Evidence of that desire surfaces in these words that He spoke to His disciples:

> I no longer call you servants, for a servant does not know what his master does. But I have called you friends, for everything that I have heard from My Father have I made known to you.[47]

What is the difference between a servant and a friend? A servant knows *what the Master requires*—the assigned task, but a true friend knows *the Master*. A true friend knows the Master's heart. Be a friend of God. He is looking for people to whom He can entrust His heart.

A Montage of this Passionate Life

What does this life of passion look like? A single snapshot of the prophetic life cannot sufficiently depict what I am trying to describe. I must show you a *montage* of images. Allow me to pull out my figurative photo album, turn the pages, point to each image and say, "*That* is what it looks like!"

---

[47] John 15:15 (MEV).

Here it is. When I am driven by a passion for Jesus, I cannot wait to worship. I am a lover of His presence, and it excites me to enter times of holy celebration with others who love His presence as deeply as I do.

When I am living with passion, I have an appetite for the Word, just as I would have an appetite for my favorite meal. Missed Bible reading time is truly missed; it makes me feel like I am starving. I have got to get into the Word!

I love the sound of His voice! I cannot wait to hear the next thing that He has to say to me. It is no burden to me to draw aside to wait and listen for Him. At the moment that He speaks, I am eager to respond and continue in conversation with Him.

I cannot wait to serve! When I serve, I enter into *His* works, and as I work, I do so in fellowship with Him. I am yoked with Him. I consider time devoted to service as time well spent with my Lord and Friend. All that I do is as worship unto Him.

Religious duty and obligation are left behind. Everything is done out of an authentic love for God. Dealing with sin is no longer about legalistically pleasing the Lord. It is more about removing anything that stands in the way of me touching His face.

Go deeper in your relationship with Jesus. Yes, be a loyal servant, but know that there is more. Be His trusted friend. Live as His faithful bride. Pursue intimacy. Seek His face, and when you find His face, gaze into His eyes. Incline your ear to His heartbeat, and let your heart-cry be like Paul's, who said, "I want to know Him!"[48] I am describing the prophetic life, and these are the characteristics of living that life with passion.

Reader's Reflections: Go to page 91 to note your reflections concerning Living with Passion. Are other things competing for your affections? Are other things threatening to extinguish your passion for Jesus? How will you address those threats? What expression of worship will you now bring to your heavenly Bridegroom? What prophetic declaration will you now make?

---

[48] Philippians 3:10.

Chapter Eight

Practices of the Prophetic Life

Over the years, God has been faithful to prepare me for a prophetic life. Here I will list a few of the things He has taught me that I think will prove helpful to you—lessons that are instructive to any who are in pursuit of the prophetic life.

1. "Keep the canvas of your mind clean. I want to paint my pictures there." The human imagination is like a canvas or a projection screen. The screen of your imagination is the same screen upon which the Holy Spirit will project visions and dreams.

Guard your thought-life. You have been given a sound, disciplined mind[49] that is capable of dwelling upon things that are true, honest, just, pure, lovely and

---

[49] 2 Timothy 1:7.

of good report.[50] Cast down any imagination that attempts to invade the sacredness of your mind.[51]

2. "Keep your tongue sanctified." The tongue that represents God must be set apart for His exclusive purposes. There are things that can defile the tongue: gossip, lying, prideful boasting, complaining, arguing, speaking in anger and the use of inappropriate language. Can both polluted and pure water flow out of the same spring?[52]

3. "Keep my secrets." Not everything that God reveals to you needs to be spoken. He is looking for someone He can trust with secrets. In prophetic ministry, the hidden things of people's lives may be revealed to you. Typically such matters are revealed for the purpose of prayer or private ministry with the person; they are not to be shared with anyone.

In the prophetic life, heaven's strategies will also be revealed to you. There is an appropriate timing and an appropriate way to unveil such things, and in some cases you are to never make them known. Wisdom from heaven is needed.

4. "Be humble and loving." Humility is a key to receiving empowering grace and favor. In more than one place, the Bible teaches that God gives grace to the

---

[50] Philippians 4:8.

[51] 2 Corinthians 10:4-5.

[52] James 3:11.

humble.[53] Fasting is a good spiritual practice that helps to renew a spirit of humility.[54]

Likewise, love is a key to activating faith. The Bible says that faith works by love.[55] If you want to function more in the prophetic and in other aspects of supernatural ministry, start doing the loving thing in the situations that you encounter. Doing acts of selfless service is a good way to ignite love.

5. "Be promptly and completely obedient." Do not delay, and do not modify what God has directed you to say or do. If it seems that you lack guidance in a situation, ask yourself, "Have I completely obeyed the last instruction the Lord has given me?" What good does it do to ask for a prophetic word when you have not responded to or acted upon the last thing He has spoken to you?

6. "Be faithful over a little." This adage is sometimes called the "little-big principle." If we are faithful over a small amount of revelation, God will entrust to us more. The way that we handle little is the same way that we will handle much. In some cases, the Lord may require a person to be faithful over

---

[53] Proverbs 3:34; James 4:6; and 1 Peter 5:5.

[54] Psalm 69:10. See J. Randolph Turpin, Jr., *21 Days of Prayer and Fasting* (Columbus, Ohio: Declaration Press, 2016).

[55] Galatians 5:6.

something that is not prophetic in nature at all as a prerequisite to being entrusted with prophetic anointing.

7. "Expect to hear my voice." Have an ear that is devoted to hearing what the Spirit is saying. Live your life every day expecting to hear His voice. Listen for Him. Learn to recognize Him. Michael Sullivant, author of *Prophetic Etiquette*, has stated, "We mustn't forget that listening, not speaking, is the basis of the prophetic."[56]

The prophet Isaiah gave testimony of God's faithfulness to speak to him, saying,

> The Sovereign Lord has given me an instructed tongue, to know the word that sustains the weary.
> He wakens me morning by morning,
> wakens my ear to listen like one being taught.[57]

This passage is so profound. Isaiah's expectation to hear the Lord speak in his waking moments not only edified him personally, but it also prepared him to be a prophetic influence in the lives of others: "to know the word that sustains the weary."

In the New Testament, James elevated the virtue of hearing or listening above the fleshly habit of

---

[56] Michael Sullivant, *Prophetic Etiquette: Your Complete Handbook on Giving and Receiving Prophecy* (Lake Mary, Florida: Charisma House, 2000), 168.

[57] Isaiah 50:4.

Practices of the Prophetic Life

undisciplined speech, stating, "Everyone should be quick to listen, slow to speak..."[58]

8. "Place a high value on what you hear." Jesus said, "Consider carefully what you hear. With the measure you use, it will be measured to you—and even more."[59] If we highly value what we hear, we will not want to ignore or forget it.

When you receive prophetic guidance or encouragement from the Lord, the first thing to do is to *believe* what you have heard. Then wisely steward every opportunity to move in the direction of the prophecy's fulfillment. Do not procrastinate regarding the word you have received. Write it down, and promptly act according to the wisdom the Spirit has given.

9. "I need you to be less concerned about being understood by others. I need you to be willing to be misunderstood." Prophetic living goes against the grain of the status quo. Prophetic people live like people who are out of synch with time; they are like time travelers from the future. When functioning in prophetic mode, future realities sometimes become so vivid that they appear to be in the present. Prophetic people see what others cannot see yet; therefore, the potential for being misunderstood by others is high. If

---

[58] James 1:19.

[59] Mark 4:24.

you become too concerned about being understood, you may shrink back from functioning prophetically. Keeping your prophetic edge requires a willingness to be misunderstood.

10. "The surest way to keep and increase whatever I give you is to give it away." Jesus said, "Freely you have received; freely give."[60] Not only are we to give our gift away by releasing prophecies to others, but we are to also impart the prophetic anointing to others, as the Spirit leads.

11. "Be passionate for my presence. I desire intimate fellowship with you." Have conversations with God. Listen more. Cultivate fellowship with the Holy Spirit. Refuse to tolerate anything that compromises or disrupts His presence in your life.

12. "Honor and celebrate the spiritual gifts and anointing of others." There is mutual benefit to honoring the gifts that others carry. When believers rightly esteem one another, it is as though a conduit opens for an exchange. Jesus said,

> "Anyone who receives a prophet because he is a prophet will receive a prophet's reward, and anyone who receives a righteous man because he is a righteous man will receive a righteous man's reward."[61]

---

[60] Matthew 10:8.

[61] Matthew 10:41.

When you honor and celebrate the prophetic gifting of others, you increase the potential of the prophetic operating in your own life.

13. "Live in the light of what I have shown you." God can show you things prophetically, but you are the one who has to live it out. Some things that He may show you will require preparation for you to receive its fulfillment. Remember that prophecies are often conditional, requiring you to meet certain conditions before you can experience the prophetic fulfillment. Start preparing. Start conducting yourself as though the fulfillment of prophetic realities were standing outside your front door. Act as though it is about to ring the door bell.

14. "Be careful of what you are allowing to shape your perception of reality." There are a lot of things competing to shape your perception of reality. Think about it. Every time you use social media, surf the web, watch the television or read the news, somebody other than you has determined what you are going to perceive. Somebody else has edited all of that content and has decided for you what you are going to know.

What is shaping your perception of reality? To live the prophetic life, we need to make sure that we are engaging the real substance of this world, such as spending face-to-face time with people and interacting with the physical world more. Even more important is the need to engage the real substance of heaven. We need to spend more time face-to-face with God, and more time listening for His voice. Let us make sure that it is *God* who is shaping our perception of reality.

Reader's Reflections: Go to page 93 to note your reflections concerning Practices of the Prophetic Life. Note a few action points for yourself—new practices that you would like to explore. Based on this exercise, what prayer do you want to pray? What prophetic declaration do you want to make?

Chapter Nine

Challenges of the Prophetic Life

What could be more exciting or more rewarding than living as a prophetic representation of Father's heart in a world needing hope? The prophetic life *is* fulfilling and empowering, yet it does have its share of challenges. Here we will note suggested ways to deal with some of them.

1. Be less concerned about being understood or accepted. This word of wisdom has already been noted. People living the prophetic life are often misunderstood. What more would you expect of a life lived on the basis of the unseen? Is it reasonable for us to expect non-prophetic people to understand those of us who hold onto future realities as though they are already fully manifested? If you set out to fully embrace the prophetic life, you will be misunderstood.

When the Lord said to me, "I need you to be less concerned about being understood by others," I came to realize that my desire for others to understand and accept me was a form of fear—a fear of man, and fear is not to rule the believer's life. Besides, if I were to modify my life for the sake of others understanding and accepting me, I would compromise my ability to influence. My life is supposed to be a sign of things not understood by natural man. My life is supposed to bring an appropriate level of prophetic tension into environments around me.

2. In the face of opposition, forgive and rejoice. The prophetic life can attract persecution. It seems to be human nature to fear what is not understood, and the fearful often attack the things they do not understand. Most times people do not realize that their attack against the prophetic is an assault against heaven, so our prayer should be the same as Jesus' when He said, "Father, forgive them, for they do not know what they are doing."[62] Other times their offense may not be quite so innocent, but even then we should heed the words of Jesus, who said,

> "Blessed are you when people insult you, persecute you and falsely say all kinds of evil against you because of me. Rejoice and be glad, because great is your reward in heaven, for in the same way they persecuted the prophets who were before you."[63]

3. When prophetic fulfillment is not in sight, remain focused on your Father's goodness. The

---

[62] Luke 23:34 (NIV).

[63] Matthew 5:11-12 (NIV).

prophetic life can have seasons of disappointment. Sometimes the prophetic person can even feel disappointed in God. If prophetic people do not properly sustain their fixation on the goodness of God, they can easily become disappointed with Him. Why would that be the case? Mike Bickle, founder of Kansas City's International House of Prayer, explains,

> They often see clearly how things should be or how God plans for them to be. But they have to wait in faith for a longer time because they have seen farther ahead. They are much more prone to the Proverbs 13:12 difficulty: "Hope deferred makes the heart sick." Because their expectations are typically higher, they are more deeply disappointed.[64]

Another way of stating this insight is that prophetic people suffer by having to live with the disparity between what "is" and what "ought" to be.

4. Encourage yourself in the Lord's presence. The prophetic life can have seasons of discouragement. Prophetic people should be the happiest people on earth, for their eyes have been opened to see things yet to come from heaven's perspective. If what they have embraced is truly a prophetic view, then their hearts should be alive with hope—an expectation of a favorable and glorious outcome. However, living with

---

[64] Mike Bickle, *Growing in the Prophetic* (Lake Mary, Florida: Creation House, 1996), 130-131.

the apparent contradiction between present realities and the prophetic future can be discouraging, especially when others refuse to see or believe what the prophetic person has seen.

Ministry leaders living a prophetic life can especially experience this challenge. If a prophetic leader becomes fixated on the present situation and dwells too much on the fact that the people he or she leads are nowhere close to their prophetic destiny, that leader can become discouraged. The disparity between what *is* and what *should be* becomes burdensome. In such times, the leader would do well to become immersed in God's presence and to be reminded of what God has said—God's promise. In the face of discouragement, declarations of God's revealed will are needed to lift the matter out of the realm of striving and elevate it to the place where it belongs—in the realm of promise. Perhaps even a faith-driven prophetic act is needed to reactivate the faith of the leader and the faith of those who follow.

Father God wants to encourage and strengthen those who represent Him. For this reason, it is critical for the prophetic life to remain centered on hosting and stewarding His presence. God's presence is the source of joy and strength. It is also important for prophetic people to not become isolated and insulated from other trusted believers through whom God might want to work to bring encouragement.

5. Keep yourself in a place of humility. Prophetic people can have a tendency to become prideful. They can have an over-realized sense of self-importance. Their personal identity can get wrapped around their gifting. Identity does not come from giftedness. Identity comes from the believer's relationship with God. Who are we? We are the sons and daughters of the Almighty. We are royalty. All of us who bear His name have been appointed to rule and reign with Him, whether we are spiritually gifted or not. We do not need to be gifted to be esteemed as significant in our Father's eyes.

Humility is greatly needed in a life characterized by the supernatural. The testimony of the Apostle Paul in Second Corinthians 12 demonstrates that God occasionally allows a "thorn in the flesh" to show up in the prophetic life.[65] In the first century world, the idiom, a "thorn in the flesh" or a "thorn in the side," referred to a person or a group of people causing irritation or even opposition. The presence of "thorns"—or trouble—reminds us of our own weaknesses and of our own great need for grace. Trouble provides an opportunity for us to be renewed in the grace of humility.

6. Remember that the prophetic is not the only important part of your life. Prophetic people can become preoccupied with the prophetic. A person can

---

[65] 2 Corinthians 12:7-10.

become so engaged with the prophetic that they neglect other vital things. In addition to the prophetic, there are the apostolic, evangelistic and pastoral aspects of the believer's life.

Mike Bickle rightly states, "Prophecy is not something in which a church should major. It's one of the many tools used to build the house, but it's not the house...."[66] He further says, "Prophetic ministry cannot be an end in itself. Its purpose is always to strengthen and promote something greater and more valuable than itself."[67]

7. Sustain an outward focus. Some prophetic communities can have the potential of becoming inwardly focused. The prophetic and the ministry of evangelism are complementary functions in the church. Although the prophetic is intended to build up the body of Christ, its purpose reaches far beyond the wellbeing of the church alone. The church exists in a world of all kinds of evil and injustices, and it exists as a prophetic community to speak into that world.

8. Hold to sound doctrine. Highly esteem the ministry of teaching. The prophetic and the ministry of teaching are complementary functions in the church. Prophetically gifted people are great at hearing the voice of God, but they are not necessarily good

---

[66] Bickle, 24-25.

[67] Ibid., 73.

exegetes. They can easily deviate from the proper interpretation of Scripture.

Insights gained prophetically for particular situations may be meant exclusively for those particular situations. They do not necessarily translate into universal principles. Taking a concept conveyed in a prophetic utterance and making an authoritative doctrine out of it would be an error. Doctrines should only rise out of a careful study of Scripture. Prophetic people need to have teachers in their lives to hold them accountable to sound biblical doctrine.

9. Recognize the need for non-prophetic people in your life. Prophetic people can underestimate the value of non-prophetic people. When prophetic people receive a word or insight from God, if they are not careful, they can have an attitude that says, "God has spoken. If you don't agree and run with the word God has spoken to me, then you are missing the will of God."

Prophetic people need to understand that they do not have the exclusive word of the Lord. Sometimes God will even speak through people who are not considered prophetic. Take for instance a case where God has prophetically shown a lead pastor that a new two-thousand seat auditorium needs to be constructed. Then the church's business manager speaks up and says, "But pastor, we don't have the assets or cash flow to justify that level of indebtedness."

The lead pastor has a choice to make. He can either label the business manager as a person full of unbelief—a person resisting the will of God for the church, or he can discern the value of having such a pragmatic individual on his team. It is not a matter of one being right and the other being wrong. In this case, both are probably right. If the lead pastor will rightly esteem the value of this non-prophetic pragmatic person, the non-prophetic person can actually help the church reach its prophetic destination. Somebody needs to be thinking budget. Somebody needs to be thinking cash flow. Somebody needs to have the freedom to say, "We have no money," without fear of being labeled a doubter. Somebody needs to be thinking about the steps needed for fulfilling the vision.

Prophetic leaders often do not see the necessary steps toward the thing that has been foreseen. Consequently, they feel tempted to create their own route, taking action in areas where they have little or no giftedness. The result can be disastrous. Other ministry gifts are needed in the process. A pragmatist can be a prophetic leader's best friend.

With all that can be said about challenges, it yet remains that a life lived in intimate communion with God supersedes any difficulty that the prophetic life may encounter. The joy of knowing the Father's heart and the privilege of walking with Him as His friend cannot be equaled. Whatever it may cost to live prophetically, it is worth it all.

Reader's Reflections: Go to page 95 to note your reflections concerning Challenges of the Prophetic Life. To which of these challenges can you relate? What additional challenges might you be facing pertaining to prophetic living? How can you best address these challenges? Based on this exercise, what prayer do you want to pray? What prophetic declaration do you want to make?

Living the Prophetic Life

Conclusion

God has placed an anointing upon you so that you might live a life that does not look like the life of everybody else. It is a life that does not blend in with a crooked, perverse and warped generation. You are one of the stars destined to shine brightly against the dark backdrop of this world.[68] Yes, you walk in this dark world, but the darkness of this world is not in you. The light and life of Jesus Christ is in you, and through you His light will shine with the brilliance of the sun. The Spirit of God is in you, and He has *anointed* you to live the prophetic life.

The past and the present do not determine your direction; you are oriented toward a hopeful future. The troubles of earth do not shake you; you are living from the vantage point of heaven. Disorder and complacency cannot remain; you are an agent of change. There is no guesswork to what you need to do;

---

[68] Philippians 2:14-15 (NIV).

Living the Prophetic Life

you are guided by revelation. You are living the prophetic life.

Yet this whole message is not about you. It is about the next person you are going to meet or touch. It is about the next conversation you are going to have. It is about the next place that you go and the next thing that you do. It is about the next prayer that you pray. In that moment, may the Holy Spirit remind you that you have been called to represent the heart and mind of the Father. You are the one who will deliver to someone and to someplace a hopeful future. You have been *appointed* to live the prophetic life.

Reader's Reflections: Go to page 97 to note your concluding reflections concerning the prophetic life. Ask Holy Spirit to guide you through the writing of a concluding prophetic declaration over your own life.

READER'S REFLECTIONS

Reflections on
The Introduction

■

Reflections on
The Prophetic Anointing

Reflections on
Living Toward the Future

Reflections on Living from Heaven

Reflections on
Living as an Agent of Change

■

Reflections on Living by Revelation

Reflections on
Living from the Future

-

Reflections on
Living with Passion

Reflections on
Practices of the Prophetic Life

Reflections on
Challenges of the Prophetic Life

Reflections on
The Conclusion

Additional Resources

Free Resources for Christian Life and Ministry

Free PDF download
21.DeclarationPress.com

Paperback: 120 pages

21 Days
of Prayer and Fasting

J. Randolph Turpin, Jr.

- What is fasting?
- Why fast? Why pray?
- How to fast
- Guidelines for congregational implementation

21 Days prepares individuals, congregations and ministry groups for extended seasons of consecration to God.

The PDF ebook edition is free. Kindle and paperback editions are also available at minimal cost. The paperback edition includes a section for journaling during the twenty-one day journey.

Free **PDF download at**
21.DeclarationPress.com

Also available in paperback, Kindle and other e-book formats.

Free Resources for Christian Life and Ministry

Free PDF download
101.DeclarationPress.com

Paperback: 90 pages

101 Prayer Models

J. Randolph Turpin, Jr.

- Jump-start your personal prayer life.
- Revitalize prayer groups and ministry teams.
- Mobilize for the ministry of prayer.

This book contains a catalog of prayer ministry models designed to involve everyone: personal and family prayer, small group prayer, congregational prayer and evangelistic prayer.

Since 1994, the author, Dr. Randy Turpin, has been training believers for the ministry of prayer. For years, he distributed handouts listing ways to cultivate a culture of prayer. In February of 2011 he compiled those lists and made them available in this publication—*101 Prayer Models*.

Free PDF download at
101.DeclarationPress.com

Also available in paperback, Kindle and other e-book formats.

Additional Ministry Resources
Available at DeclarationPress.com

DeclarationPress.com

Paperback: 150 pages

Prayer Strategy
A Planning Workbook

J. Randolph Turpin, Jr.

PRAYER STRATEGY facilitates a team approach to developing the ministry of prayer. The workbook is formatted as a retreat guide, but it can also be used in other settings.

Part 1 is a guide for an initial orientation, a personal prayer inventory and a congregational assessment.

Part 2 directs the team through four steps of a 5-step planning process.

Part 3 guides the final step in the 5-step process: work the plan. Through a series of follow-through meetings, the team pursues the goals set during the planning retreat.

Available at DeclarationPress.com

DeclarationPress.com

Paperback: 314 pages

Behold the Son
A Study of the Gospel of John

J. Randolph Turpin, Jr.

BEHOLD THE SON has been prepared as a resource for personal study and as a tool for teachers walking their students through a study of the Gospel of John. These pages contain the complete text of the Gospel According to John. The commentary in the footnotes features technical notes, cross references, sermon notes and the author's personal reflections. To further assist in the study, tables have been inserted providing a harmony of the Gospels in those places where such information might prove relevant and helpful.

Dr. Turpin declares this blessing over all who work through this study: "May you behold the Son of God with every turn of the page, with every word that you ponder, and with every prayer that you pray in response to the message of this amazing Gospel."

Available at DeclarationPress.com

Shared Discernment

A Workbook for Ministry Planning Teams

J. Randolph Turpin, Jr.

DeclarationPress.com

Paperback: 192 pages

SHARED DISCERNMENT guides teams through a planning process involving *listening* for the Spirit's voice, *sharing* what has been heard and *discerning* what it means.

This workbook is designed for use in retreat or planning settings.

Part 1 explains the 4 phases of the discernment process.

Part 2 guides an initial orientation.

Part 3 covers 4 of 5 steps: assess, set goals, plan a course of action and agree/celebrate.

Part 4 covers step 5—Work the Plan. Through follow-through meetings and projects, the team pursues its goals.

Available at DeclarationPress.com

For more, go to
DeclarationPress.com

www.ingramcontent.com/pod-product-compliance
Lightning Source LLC
Chambersburg PA
CBHW071300040426
42444CB00009B/1802